إسمي غابريالا، تحبُ أسرتي أكلَ خبزِ الفاهيتا الساخنِ مع الفلفل.
هذا لذيذٌ! إنهُ طبقي المفضلْ!

My name's Gabriela. My family loves eating hot, spicy chilli and fajitas.

Yum

Yum

Yummy!

My favourite!

# لذّةٌ، هذا لذيذٌ! لنأكلْ!

# Yum! Let's Eat!

Thando Maclaren
Illustrated by Jacqueline East

Arabic translation by Wafa' Tarnowska

3 8002 02334 196 1

أنا ماريا و أمي تطهي المعكرونةَ
بالخضار.
هذا لذيذٌ ! إنهُ طبقي المفضلْ!

I'm Maria and my mama's
making pasta primavera.

Yum

Yum

Yummy!

My favourite!

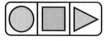

إسمي خالد. نحنُ نأكلُ الكوسكوسْ وطاجينْ لحمِ الغنمِ عندما نزورُ جدّي. هذا لذيذٌ! انهُ طبقي المفضلْ!

I'm Khaled. We eat cous cous and lamb tagine when we visit Grandpa.

Yum
    Yum
        Yummy!

My favourite!

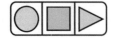

أنا أغاتا، جدُّتي تحضرُ يخنةَ البيغوس المميزةِ لي ولأختي.
هذا لذيذٌ! إنهُ طبقي المفضلْ!

My name's Agata. My granny is making her special bigos for me and my big sister.

Yum
   Yum
      Yummy!

My favourite!

أنا دواين وأحبُ أكلَ الأرزِ والبازيلا مع كاري لحمِ الماعز.
هذا لذيذٌ! انهُ طبقي المفضلْ!

I'm Dwayne and I love eating rice and peas with goat curry.

Yum

Yum

Yummy!

My favourite!

إسمي يمين. أمي تحضرُ الدجاجَ المقليِ
والذرةِ الصغيرةِ على الطريقة الصينية.
هذا لذيذٌ! إنهُ طبقي المفضلْ!

My name's Yi-Min. My mum is making
stir fry with chicken and baby corn.

Yum

Yum

Yummy!

My favourite!

أنا أبيبا. تحبُ أسرتي أكلَ خبزِ الانجير
امع يخنةِ اللحمِ الحرة. هذا لذيذٌ!
إنهُ طبقي المفضلْ!

I'm Abeba and my family loves
eating injera with spicy zigni.

Yum
    Yum
        Yummy!

My favourite!

إسمي أيكو. أنا أكلُ المعكرونةَ وسمكَ السوشي النيِّ معَ أخي وأختي.
هذا لذيذٌ! إنهُ طبقي المفضلْ!

My name's Aiko. I'm eating noodles and sushi with my brother and sister.

Yum
  Yum
    Yummy!

    My favourite!

أنا بريتي وجدتي تحضرُ العدسَ وخبزَ
الروتي لي ولأبي لنأكلهما مع شرابِ
اللبنِ والمانغا .
هذا لذيذٌ! انهُ طبقي المفضلْ!

I'm Priti and my granny makes
dhal and roti, with mango lassi
for me and daddy.

Yum

    Yum

        Yummy!

My favourite!

أنا تشارلي وأنا أكلُ فطيرةَ اللحمِ مع الخضرةِ والبطاطا مع أمي وأبي.
هذا لذيذٌ! انهُ طبقي المفضلْ!

My name's Charlie. I'm having shepherd's pie with Mum and Dad.

Yum
Yum
Yummy!
My favourite!

إسمي ياسين. أحبُ أكلَ الكباب وورقِ العريشِ المحشي بالأرزِ مع أبي وأخي الكبير!

هذا لذيذٌ! انهُ طبقي المفضلْ!

I'm Yasin and I love eating kebabs and dolma with Daddy and my big brother!

Yum
   Yum
      Yummy!

My favourite!

Turkey

Poland

India

Mexico

Jamaica

Japan

Italy

Morocco

Ethiopia

UK

China